THE BEAUTY OF THE BROKEN

KATHY BIGGERS

KSB Productions

ISBN: 9798589432909

Cover design by: Art Painter
Library of Congress Control Number: 2018675309
Printed in the United States of America

I dedicate this work to my precious family: my so supportive husband, Steve, my mother, Betty Lewis, my daughter and her husband, Amanda and Jason Blair, my adorable granddaughters, Courtney and Madison, and, especially, my late father, Derrel Lewis, Th.D., who enjoined me, on his deathbed, to finish this work! God has blessed me much more than I deserve with these people!

CONTENTS

INTRODUCTION

Dear Reader:

The following has been running through my head and my heart for years. God has been moving me to share these things and I have made several false starts, experienced countless delays, and generally put this off. I had almost wrapped it up, put a bow on it and shipped it off until my sweet daughter read it and said that there was something missing.

What was missing was that I wasn't yet broken enough. Apparently, our nation was not broken enough. I thought we were. I thought that I had thoroughly been run through the wringer and come out the other side and was ready to share. I thought, after riots and shootings and national upheaval, there wasn't much more that could happen. I was wrong. There was more to come.

I know the message. The Father made it clear to me long ago. I also know that this message has been articulated in multiple formats by multiple people over multiple years. I have only my experience to add to the plethora of studies out there and my experience is not unusual. Many times, I have asked the Father what reason anyone might have to consider my poor additions. I think the very existence of that question contains the answer. I have nothing new. I have nothing, period. But God does. When He instigates a task, He has an end result. As I move through this process, I experience His leading and healing. That, alone, is enough end result for His children. We have to know that the Father knows His plan for us and that His plans are never empty, never pointless, and never without reward. My prayer is that the reader will experience a new understanding of how great is the Father's love and His work in the most broken places of our lives. May He show His presence, mercies, grace and purpose in a fresh new way as we undertake how God moves in the broken places of our lives.

In His love,

Kathy Biggers

Broken Pieces

Have you failed in life's battles to accomplish your
plan?
Is your heart heavy, laden, do you fear the Lords'
command?
Do you feel that no one loves you and there's no
use to try?
Just bring your cares to Jesus. Your soul He'll
satisfy.

Chorus
Pick up the broken pieces and bring them to the
Lord.
Pick up the broken pieces, trust in His Holy word.
He will put you back together and make your life
complete.
Just place the broken pieces at the Saviors feet.

Bill Gaither

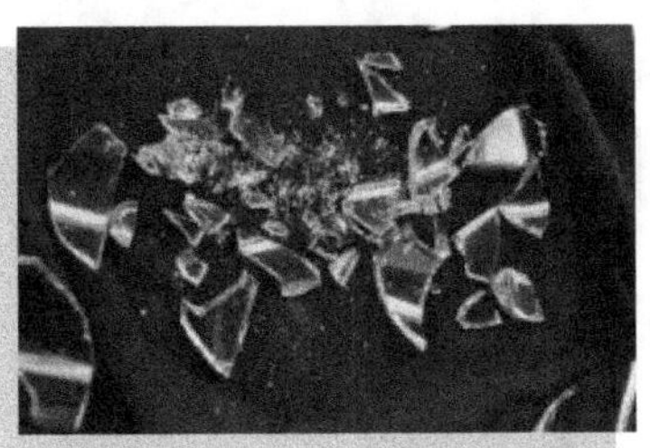

THERE IS BEAUTY IN THE BROKEN THINGS

Each of us, if we have lived more than a minute, has felt that we'd reached the end of our rope. We've dealt with broken hearts, scraped knees, wounded spirits and wounded minds. We've dealt with financial failures, serious illnesses, career failures, and the death of loved ones. We've watched our government, our healthcare industry, and our societies as they crumble around us. It seems that life is shattering. That we are shattering.

In whatever manner that you're broken and shattered, is it the end? Do you think you're irreparable? Forever damaged? Are you trying to eke out a life while you hide your pain and brokenness behind a mask (figuratively or literally)? Or can true beauty arise out of the broken places?

It can. The Japanese have a centuries-old art form known as "kintsugi," which, so appropriately, translates as "Golden Journey.´ In this "golden journey," broken porcelain or pottery is repaired with a special lacquer mixed with gold, silver or platinum. The result is not only a beautiful piece of art but one that is stronger than the original piece.

God has a Golden Journey for you. More than a Golden Journey. More than you can imagine. As Paul said in I Corinthians 2:9, "Eye has not seen, nor ear heard, nor has entered into the heart of man the things which God has prepared for those who love Him."

You need to know that God doesn't ignore your pain. In fact, He hurts that His children hurt. He loves YOU and it hurts that YOU hurt, and He wants to bring good for you out of everything that you go through.

That is why He sent His only Son, Jesus Christ. The one verse from the Bible that most who know anything about it can quote is, "For God so loved the **world** that He gave His one and only Son that whoever believes in Him should not perish but have eternal life." (John 3:16 New International Version) Jesus came willingly (see John 16 and 17) so that we could live. So that we could live "abundantly," to the fullest potential for which He created us. (John 10:10) During His time on earth, Jesus reached out and touched those who hurt and, when the burden of death, sin and doubt were hammered home for Him at the death of his friend, Lazarus, "Jesus wept." (John 11:35)

I pray that the following chapters will help you see how much Jesus wants to reach you and make your brokenness into your beauty. How much you are loved, even when you feel beaten, broken and unloved.

God has said ..."I have loved you with an everlasting love; I have drawn you with unfailing kindness. ..."

Jeremiah 31:3b

<u>REFLECTION TIME</u>

On these pages, you will be able to sit back and think of ways the previous chapter applies in your life. This is yours. It is personal and you should feel free to insert whatever is in your heart.

For now, think about your purpose. Do you know that you have a purpose for being on this earth? You do.

- What is your reason for living? (Don't give up, it's there. If you don't know yet, hang in there.)

- What gives you the most joy in your life?

- Most heartache?

NOTES

DEFINITELY BROKEN

At the time I had "completed" this the first time, we were still mourning that, on Sunday, November 5, 2017, 26 year old Devin Patrick Kelly stormed a small Baptist Church in beautiful, rural Sutherland Springs, Texas. He unleashed a fury of gunfire as he stalked up and down the center aisle. 26 people were killed and 20 more were wounded, including a baby, young children, a pregnant mom, a family and the aged. Reports are that he was screaming, "Everybody dies, (epithet deleted)!"

That has long ago faded from the news cycle and stands out in my mind as part of the first salvos of brokenness. Unless you had relatives involved, it may have faded from your mind. **But it was very strong evidence that something is radically broken!!!!!**

Since that time, so much has occurred. A "novel" virus burst onto the scene under suspicious circumstances and put the globe under house arrest. Fear invaded our communities as "experts" wavered in the correct behavior, the correct demeanor, the correct attitude. We were isolated from our communities, our families, and our churches. The media kept the terror heightened by trumpeting growing numbers of cases and deaths. Social media and state and local officials promoted neighbor-against-neighbor arguments and "snitching" against behavioral "transgressors" while, in the meantime, families lost jobs and business, their very livelihood. Suicide and domestic abuse rates climbed. Hopelessness pervaded.

Then we watched in shock as George Floyd was killed before our very eyes and were mired in confusion when the autopsy reports and additional footage contradicted our every thought. We followed daily, in horror, as Antifa and Black Lives Matter moved forward into a crisis situation to propel the United States and the world into utter chaos, murder and destruction. We were stunned at the "live" filming of the murder of retired St. Louis police captain David Dornan while this wonderful black man was murdered by "Black Life Matters" thugs.

We have endured lockdowns, quarantines, illness and botched elections. As of this writing, the destruction of society is continuing unabated and an anti-human, anti-God culture is raging across the globe.

An earlier Time Magazine blog stated, "If you could see grief on a map, there would be rings of anguish radiating from whole regions of the U.S. right now." (Time.com, 2017) A map of brokenness. The stories of tragedies, terror attacks, beheadings, wars and rumor of wars indicate that this map should radiate around the whole earth, indeed becoming a solid mass versus "rings of anguish."

We are hit weekly by national and international, personal and interpersonal tragedies to the point that we cry out, "HOW??? WHY???" Increasing multitudes are asking, "If there is a God, how can this be? How can the world be so broken? How can my family be so broken? <u>How can I be so broken?</u>"

Those who would never ask questions about the existence of God are, if honest, asking, "If we're evolving from beasts, then how is it that we see fellow men becoming more and more beastly". Isn't that **devolving**?

For believer and unbeliever alike, I'm going to share a little secret. Jesus, Himself, told those absolutely closest to Him, "In this world you **will have tribulation!**" (John 16:33 KJV) He warned them: it's going to happen. **The world is broken.**

Now, why would the Son of the Living God toss such negativity out to his closest and most beloved? Didn't He say that He came that we might have abundant life? (John 10:10b) Yes. Undeniably, yes! He has a purpose for you and he wants **your** life to be full and abundant!!!

But why, then, could "abundant life" contain so much pain and fear? Why is anger and hurt so widespread? Why is it that I hurt so much? Why can't I help those I love? **What's "abundant" about this?**

If you will bear with me, we will dig into that question and what it means and where it leads. The pain we see, the pain we experience in this life right now, has **eternal meaning**, from what we see as the beginning to what we see as the end.

And, if we can be honest with each other, if I can be honest with myself, we can begin to see God more clearly. We can see Him working in us. And we can see ourselves as He sees us.

And we can know, YOU can know, that He, the Master of all, wants to take all of our broken pieces and make them into a beautiful Kintsugi! Because He has called us! He has called YOU to be an indispensible part of His plan for the world!!!

<u>REFLECTION TIME</u>:

- What would "abundant life" look like to you?

- Are you assured that you were put here with purpose?

- Do you have any inkling what your purpose(s) may be?

NOTES

THE SETUP

Romans 8:22 tells us, "We know that the whole creation has been groaning as in the pains of childbirth right up to the present time."

If you're a guy, this has little meaning to you. There's an amusing internet meme that states, "During labor, the pain is so great that I can almost imagine what it feels like when a man has a cold." Somewhat humorous, right? I don't mean to denigrate the pains that men have felt because they can be intense; my own husband has broken his spine in two places and still has occasional pain from the experience, although, through the grace of God and against all odds, he can walk and function at very high capacity.

I understand that kidney stones may be extraordinarily painful, and they are often compared to being in labor. But, frankly, labor, the pain of childbirth, is different. No doubt, **labor hurts**. I only have one daughter but I was in hard, every five minute labor for eighteen hours. I breathed and I hurt, but I knew I had a baby coming, so it was worth it. Mothers, those hours or moments when the body is wracked with imploding and intense contractions and each breath is impossible but comes anyway, can that compare with anything else? And the primary differentiator between labor and **any other pain** is the end result. Labor is designed to bring forth life. Each pang has a purpose. In our broken world, we sometimes don't get to see and hold that bit of eternal life on **this** plane, but labor brings forth life. Life with purpose. Life with a plan. Even the most damaged little person brought forth has a purpose and a plan.

I had the joy of seeing the beautiful little girl who was the end result of my labor. Many women go through the labor and don't get to see that life. I can imagine much that would be more painful … far more than physical pain. It is difficult to imagine how beauty could possibly come out of that pain. How can beauty come out of the despair when one loses a child? Can there be purpose after such agony?

Well, difficult though it is to imagine, yes. The depths of despair can, indeed, result in eternal and exquisite loveliness. Life, with all its beauty and all of its pain. Its ups and downs. The moments of darkness that we each go through, to some degree, can feel like labor. Are the pangs bringing forth anything good? If labor brings forth life, is there something good coming forth out of the dark moments of our life? Does it even have meaning???

YES! God designed His creation with a purpose and a plan. Before the creation of this earth, God had designed a heavenly family and counsel. As he spoke the world into existence, He purposed to express and demonstrate more of who He is. As He spoke man into existence, He expressed more of Himself than ever before. As His human creation chose disobedience and self-imposed separation from his Creator, God already had a plan in place to redeem, to restore and to perfect His creation. God sent His Only Son, Jesus, second person of the eternal Trinity by whom all things are held together, to shoulder our brokenness, sacrifice Himself, and rise again. Restoration complete, though not yet realized until His return. In every step of this, God has revealed more and more of Himself. Purpose. Plan.

So, how does the shattering we see in the world, the pain we experience in our lives, reflect purpose and a plan? Or does it matter? And, if you're hurting, WHAT DIFFERENCE DOES IT MAKE TO YOU?

It matters. It matters tremendously to God when you hurt. Dr. Adrian Rogers wrote:

"After Adam and Eve sinned, after the infection and sickness of sin came into this world, God said to them, "Cursed is the ground for thy sake..." (Genesis 3:17). He didn't say, "for your punishment," but, "for your sake, for your welfare." The worst thing that could have happened would have been for them to have lived in paradise with a sinful nature and be immune to pain, because pain is the signal that something is wrong and needs to be fixed." (https://www.christianity.com/christian-life/spiritual-growth/the-purpose-of-pain-11599385.html)

So, from our forefathers on, we are broken. There's no denying it. If you will walk to your mirror, look yourself in the eye and be honest, you will have to say, "I'm broken." I've known my inadequacies, and they are many, for a long time. I even chose my degree and my graduate studies in psychology largely to try to understand my own shortcomings and some of the lousy choices I had made.

Some breaks look bigger than others. Some breaks just look like small cracks. Some have become huge injuries that have grown and accumulated over a lifetime. Some hurt worse than others. But we're all broken.

You may have navigated a successful career and gained (or gained, lost and gained again) millions of dollars, or you may be a stay-at-home parent whose children are moving through the phases of needing you and are becoming their own little broken people and you are discovering that you can't fix the pains and broken places that are part of their growing up. You may pastor a large, successful church or you may have no idea what God wants you to be when you grow up (even if you're already at retirement age). You may have been imprisoned by adultery, prostitution, addiction, pornography, abuse and other heinous states of being.

You may already know that God has a purpose for your life or maybe you don't know for sure if there even is a God. The truth is, even though we have so many questions and so few answers, even though we are broken people, <u>God wants us, loves us, and wants us to be whole, to be His!</u>

So, "the whole creation has been groaning as in the pains of childbirth right up to the present time." The total brokenness of creation, the total brokenness of EACH OF US, is laboring RIGHT NOW till God brings us to the time that we are whole in His presence. We start now.

<u>The Evidence of Brokenness Around Us</u>

Even before the "world went mad" around us at the breakout of a pandemic and the racial and political unrest that erupted, unfettered and brutal, onto the globe, there was abundant evidence of that brokenness all around us. The underlying political unrest bursting outward in violence, family breakdown followed by parentless homes, divorce, drug and alcohol usage, general societal malaise, personal pain and fear – all these are evidence of how badly we're broken.

Statistics are loud indicators of the problem. In the United States, major diagnosed depression affects over 40 million adults, over 18% of the population of the U.S. at a cost of more than $42 billion per year. In 2016, suicide rates surged to a 30 year high and a noticeable increase was among women and teenagers. In fact, suicide is the **second leading cause of death among teenagers and preteens and third for children ages 5 years to 10 years!!!!** (http://jasonfoundation.com/prp/facts/youth-suicide-statistics/) These are symptoms of severe brokenness!

But these are the big symptoms. What about what **you** feel? What does your daughter or son feel? Your mother or father? Your spouse. Your cousins/friends/co-workers/fellow church-goers? Is there anyone of your acquaintance who is stellarly complete and perfect and whole???? Honestly?? **Absolutely not!**

It is so easy to perceive wholeness and near-perfection in some of those around us. The beautiful actress who knows Jesus and has multiple national speaking ministries (there are more of these women than you think), is she unbroken? No. If you ask her, she can tell you of the many ways she failed to live up to her own standards, much less those of the Lord. (I was originally going to add "of Hollywood," but I believe it's evident that Hollywood *has no standards*.) She may tell you about her divorces, her abortions, her clashes with "the casting couch."

The preacher's wife? They're always pretty close to perfect, right? Well, my mother would beg to differ. It has been a great challenge to her to be the introverted background to my father's ministry and then the caregiver to him as his health failed and then his widow as he passed. It has been a great challenge and joy to her to find God's purpose for her now that she is no longer "the preacher's wife."

The singer, performer, comedian, comedienne? Ask them. The answer is nope.

The preacher's kid (me)? Well, of course not!! We all know the answer to that! Just ask the deacon's kids! Kidding aside, I can testify to the difficulties my two brothers and I experienced as PKs. My own journey involved a long descent into eating disorders and relationship issues. My younger brother, the middle child, became a drug addict who struggled long and hard with recovery. The "baby brother" is a preacher and I'm very proud of him, but he has had his own health issues throughout life. We are not atypical of pastors' families at all, and, as we discuss the invisible enemy of all humans, I can attest that the enemy is exceptionally focused on the families of those who serve God.

Scripture tells us that we're all broken! "All have sinned and come short of the glory of God." (Romans 3:23). "There is none that does good: no, NOT ONE!" (Romans 3:12) I think that I can safely say that most of us TRY to do good. We TRY to BE good. But, if you're like me (and you are), you will be honest and say that it's never enough. I'm never enough. We are never enough. So where do we go from here?

Well, I have a lot of questions and some answers, but I know The One who has all of the answers and, in His kindness and grace, He didn't leave us hanging. So I'd like to invite you to share some of the questions, some of the problems, and where we begin to find the answers to where we go from here. God has promised His beauty out of our brokenness. Let's find out how.

<u>REFLECTION TIME</u>

As you move through this with me, I'm going to ask you to ask yourself some questions. I am in hopes that these might lead each of us to a better understanding of ourselves and our purposes. Questions in each "reflection" section are for your personal journey. These may be discussed in small groups if you are comfortable with that, but that is not necessary. This is for you.

If you are moving through this with a small group, I pray that these questions will lead to transparency, understanding and deeper friendships.

- Have you ever felt like you were just "not enough" in a given situation?

- What are some examples of times when you were aware of your own inadequacy?

- What was your response in those times?

- What/who helped you move through those times?

- Did you have any spiritual and/or scriptural influence that gave you peace or comfort?

SO WHAT'S THE PROBLEM WITH ME?

The first step in becoming more than a broken vessel is looking inward. All the statistics in the world don't matter, the broken state of others doesn't matter, and none of it matters unless I can look in the mirror and SEE ME! And you can do the same.

As I state above, I have long said that I don't believe there is a woman alive who believes that she is "enough." I can't speak for men, but I do know my dad's heart and I know that he felt that same deficit until his death. My husband has occasionally expressed a similar thought.

Christian comedienne Chonda Pierce, in her movie, *"Enough,"* points out that we often look to our family, our church, our job, our WHATEVER to help us feel like we might be enough, because we don't think we ARE enough. Chonda points out that Christ's sacrifice for us demonstrates that we ARE enough. Though I love her message here, I have to respectfully disagree with the primary point. We are NOT enough. We are loved and JESUS is enough, so he transforms us to HIS "enough".

For years, as I've lived in my head with this *Beauty of the Broken* content, I've known that we CAN NEVER BE enough. It's a little silly example, but I look back on the first time I gave my little two-year old daughter "fruit at the bottom" yogurt and, having never seen it before, looked at the top and asked her why she had spit in it! I'll never forget the hurt and indignation in those beautiful little eyes as she informed me that she never did such a thing!! I stirred the carton, discovered the logistics and apologized but, to this day, decades later, still get a sinking feeling in my heart when I think of the hurt in those eyes! I wasn't "enough" to protect my little girl's heart in the silliest, most trivial of matters! From me! (In my defense, "fruit at the bottom" had just come out and NO ONE in the marketplace had ever seen it before, but I digress.)

There were those moments, days, hours, and months that I didn't know how to be enough of a mother to my daughter while her father and I divorced. There are still those moments when I don't know how to be enough to help her navigate the shoals along her journey as a Christian wife and mom and chronic illness sufferer.

As a wife, I can look back on too many times that my attitude, my responses, my love or lack thereof demonstrate the number of ways that mark my lack of "enoughness" as a wife/friend to the wonderful husband that God has given me.

As a daughter, I have too many stories to tell where I failed or didn't quite do enough for my wonderful parents. As my dad went into hospice for his final days and we gathered around him, I lamented that I had not asked more questions, listened to more stories, spent more time. As he shared with me his heart for my future and his desire that I finish certain things, including this book, and that I take his unfinished manuscripts and work on them, I longed for more time to work WITH him on those things. It was just NOT ENOUGH!!! <u>I had not been enough!</u>

I think back to the months that my husband and I spent travelling as I sang and spoke throughout the country with our little ministry and remember all of those beautiful people who came to me after and shared their hearts and their pains and longings and I don't believe there is any way that I can ever feel that I gave them enough. Enough of myself. Enough of my heart. Enough "right answers." ENOUGH OF JESUS!

I've suggested that men aren't any different in that. I've listened to the stories and regrets of men I have known, and, when they are honest, men will tell you that they, too, don't believe that they are "enough." My dad had one of the most impactful ministries anyone has seen and he confessed to me, toward the end, that he felt like a failure. Now I'm a "seasoned citizen," and I understand what he meant. So many lost opportunities and "wasted" time that nothing feels like ENOUGH!

Let's face it, we're right! WE ARE JUST NOT ENOUGH! We come to our life's moments, life's relationships, broken and a clueless. We don't possess the ability, within ourselves, to even fix ourselves, to even help ourselves adequately. So now what?

<u>REFLECTION TIME</u>

- What are some examples of a broken world that I see around me on the day that I am reading this?

- Who are the people who depend on me? Am I confident I am enough for them?

- Am I broken? Do I look at myself every day and feel that I can do and be everything that is required of me?

- Do I have "big deal injuries," those things that have occurred at any time in the past and still cause me pain? (Maybe these are not huge but they hurt.)

- Are there any "cracks" in my life? The smaller, "not quite right" things?

- What are the things that make me feel most overwhelmed?

- Who would I really like to be? (This one is hard, so don't get hung up on it.)

- Am I ready to look at the places that I feel most broken and see what God can do?

- Do I really believe that these are important in the eternal scheme of things? To an eternal God?

Reflection verses:

"There is none righteous; no, not one." Romans 3:10

Humans are broken!

"The Lord is near to the brokenhearted and saves the crushed in spirit." Psalm 34:13

God gets it.

"For thus says the One who is high and lifted up, who inhabits eternity, whose name is Holy: 'I dwell in the high and holy place, <u>and also with him who is of a contrite and lowly spirit, to revive the spirit of the lowly, and to revive the heart of the contrite.'"</u> Isaiah 57:15

God cares and He is waiting on you. He wants you. He loves you.

BEGIN AT THE BEGINNING:

BROKEN, LOST and ALONE

Caroline came to in her pickup truck. The nose of the truck was pointing down into the ravine. Caroline was on the passenger side, face in the seat, almost in a prayerful position, when she regained consciousness. She looked to her right and was stunned to find that the driver's seat, which she had occupied, was now being crushed by the steering wheel. She couldn't fathom how she had escaped the crush and been moved to the passenger seat.

Her entire body hurt and she realized that she could barely move. Where was she? What had happened? Why was she here? She realized that she had no clue about why her pickup was crushed, who had been involved, if anyone else had been hurt. She knew she had been high. Had she killed someone? Maimed someone? Terrified, Caroline moved to the passenger door and, finds that she could push it open, fell to the ground. She looked up and could see nothing but trees. She looked down and around. Trees. She had no clue where she was, but there was no one around. Just trees.

As Caroline maneuvered to a standing position, she realized that she couldn't make her legs work. She could stand, but not walk, not pull forward. Not knowing if she had just then been in a wreck or if she had been there for some time, she feared that the truck might blow up at any moment. Trying to thrust forward, she found herself lying on the side of the ravine. She lay facing the sky, totally at the end of herself. She knew that her phone was where it always was, in the console between the driver and passenger seat, so she knew she couldn't call anyone.

A little backstory - Caroline had left her mother's home twenty years earlier. She lived totally outside "the system," no driver's license, no social security card, no proof she existed. She recounts how she stole everything that she "owned." She was an angry girl who grew into an angry woman. For twenty years, she had lived on the streets or in someone else's place. She had hung with the city's gangs and been involved in prostitution, drugs, both using and selling, theft and everything that one might think a gang member might do. She had a daughter, but she had never made any effort to be a mother to that daughter. She had a grandchild, but she was not allowed to be anywhere near the child.

Now, Caroline was alone. Totally alone. Totally broken, body and soul. And she was afraid.

Caroline thought there was a God. She thought that He was totally unfair and had given her a raw deal and she was mad at Him. But now she was alone. Now she had no one else. In desperation, she looked up at the sky and said, "God, I don't understand. I don't know what's happening. I don't know. But I need you. I need you, I need Jesus, I need that other one … I don't remember His name! (Holy Spirit) But I need you to come help me understand. And, if you can make me understand, if you can help me, I'm your's. I'm yours forever."

Lots of people make "get out of jail" a promise to God, but Caroline was totally honest. She knew that she hadn't become anything that God should hear, but she wanted Him now. And she felt Him "come down." At that moment, since He obviously heard her, she gave her entire being to the Lord.

Caroline describes a sudden peace in her heart, a peace so unfamiliar that she reached up to her chest and laid her hand on her heart … and felt a lump in her pocket. Her phone! She never had her phone on her when driving, but here it was! Was it damaged in the accident?

With trembling, she reached in her pocket and pulled out her phone. The signal was very weak, but there it was! Caroline wracked her brain to decide who to call. No one would care, would they? She couldn't call 911; what if she had inadvertently killed someone! Plus, she had no idea of her location!! So she called the next best person, the most connected person in the entire metroplex area, the head of the most powerful gang. When he answered, she gave him a rundown as best she could and was stunned when he said, "I can't help you!"

"What do you mean you can't help me?"

"Girl, I don't know where you are and I ain't got no way to find you!! You gotta call 911!"

"I can't! They may be looking for me!"

"Well, that's the only way. They can find you." And he hung up.

Caroline lay there for a moment starting at the sky, still feeling that God was there with her. So she dialed 911. When the dispatcher asked her location, she told her that all she could see was trees and the sky and somewhere up higher was the top of the hill. The dispatcher instructed her to walk to the top.

"I CAN'T WALK. I CAN'T WALK!"

The dispatcher calmly told her, "You stay on the phone with me and you hold that phone up as high as you can. Hold it up and we'll find you." Within a short while, Caroline heard a siren. Then she saw faces peering down, exclaiming, "Holy smokes!!!!" The officers scrambled down and moved to each side, telling her to stay calm and they would help her walk up. Not possible. Caroline's legs wouldn't move.

Then paramedics arrived and they carried her to the road on a stretcher and loaded her into an ambulance. Wracked with pain and filled with fear, Caroline made the ambulance journey to the emergency room, not knowing what they might possibly do with her at the hospital. As far as society and the government were concerned, she didn't exist. No driver's license, no social security card, Caroline had been "off the radar" for more than twenty years. She didn't know if any hospital would even treat her.

But treat her they did. Caroline's hip was crushed and she was admitted and treated immediately. As she improved, she lay in the hospital bed wondering what was next and where she would go when discharged. She would be in a wheelchair for some time and she was totally homeless and without connections.

As she lay staring at the ceiling, a nurse entered and informed her, "Your daughter is here?"

"My daughter?!? What is she doing here???"

"She's here to see you. Can she come in?"

Her daughter was a near stranger to her. She thought again about how her own behavior had resulted in banishment from her daughter's home and total estrangement from her grandson. She had been the worst mother possible. She knew it. She had treated her child horribly. Had that child come to gloat? Well, she deserved the chance, and Caroline was determined to make a new start, since God had been faithful to answer her, and to see her daughter.

She was totally unprepared for her daughter's kindness!

"Mama, I'm going to take you home with me." Home!? She had been banished. She would be totally at the mercy of someone who absolutely deserved revenge. But what else could she do? Through her fear, Caroline looked into her daughter's eyes and was stunned that she saw caring. She saw that someone wanted to take care of her. She saw that she might now have a home.

Over the weeks and months of healing, Caroline's daughter faithfully witnessed to her of God's love and began to teach her mother about how God's children demonstrated love. Caroline began to attend church and learned that the people there were not "holier than thou" hypocrites but caring believers who wanted to walk with her and hold her up as she learned to be more of what God wanted her to be. She learned faithfulness. She learned that the Father God answered her prayers, even if they weren't "rescue me" prayers! Even when the Lord provided a new home far from anyone she knew, she learned to trust Him and she gained a whole new family of believers who would walk alongside her and love her. She learned that God is love and that He had provided for her and had been there in her life long before she recognized Him.

Caroline went from alone and broken to NEVER being alone, because the Father was ready to hear her prayer and fill her broken loneliness. He gave her a life!

If you haven't looked to Him yet for life, please know that:

"[11]And this is the testimony: God has given us eternal life, and this life is in His Son. [12] The one who has the Son has life. The one who doesn't have the Son of God does not have life. [13] I have written these things to you who believe in the name of the Son of God, so that you may know that you have eternal life." (1 John 5:11-13)

REFLECTION TIME

- Refer back to the old questions the Quakers would ask: if you were to die tonight, where would you go?

- If you were to die tonight and God were to ask you, "Why should I let you in to my heaven?" what would say?

Let's keep going.

NO, NEVER ALONE AGAIN!

How do you check this out? Well, a very "religious" leader came to Jesus during His time here on earth and began to question Him.   During that question period, Jesus gave Him that precious assurance:

"God so loved that world that He gave His only Son that who-ever believes in Him **will not perish but have eternal life.** For God did not send His Son into the world that He might con-demen the world, but that the world might be saved **through Him.**" (John 3:16-17)

God, who really does love THAT MUCH, does not make this difficult for anyone who will examine His claims and His truths and will call on Him.

For <u>whoever</u> will call on the name of the Lord will be saved."
- Romans 10:13

How You Can Know God's Love

Here is some serious love! Romans 5:8 tells us that God loved us so that "when we were in our sin, Christ Jesus came to die for us."

Who, me? Romans 3:23 says "for all have sinned and fall short of the glory of God,"

We know that. We know that, as much as we like to think, "Well, I'm a good person," we're not all that different from Caroline. We can spot our flaws. We curse. We hate people. We feel sorry for ourselves. We feel road rage. We make excuses for bad behavior. We know that we don't measure up.

We fall short of what He intended for our lives to be. He intended for us to know Him, to receive His love and to love Him. To be all that He created us to be!

But He loves us enough to allow us to choose. We are made "in His Image" and that requires that we have choice, as He has choice. We can stay self-absorbed and live with our desires ... and our lonely brokenness ... and be separated from Him and His love. That is sin. And we die.

Romans 6:23:"For the wages of sin is death, but the free gift of God is eternal life in Christ Jesus our Lord."

In other words, we get what we've asked for ... separation from God. Which is death, alone and dark. God's free gift is life. He paid for your life with death on the cross and resurrection TO life and He offers it. And, as 2 Peter 3:9 tell us, He "is patient toward you, not wishing for **ANY** to perish but for all to come to repentance."

> **Such love!** Second Corinthians 5:21 says, "He who knew no sin became sin for us, that we may be made the righteousness of God through Him."

Jesus arose from the grave to conquer sin and death

for all who receive Him as God's free gift.

for all who receive Him as God's free gift.

REFLECTION TIME

DON'T SKIP THIS ONE!!!!

How can you receive God's free gift of love and life?

Romans 10:9-10 "that if you confess with your mouth Jesus as Lord, and believe in your heart that God raised Him from the dead, you will be saved; for with the heart a person believes, resulting in righteousness, and with the mouth he confesses, resulting in salvation."

A person receives God's free gift of love and life by placing faith in Jesus Christ. To believe is simply to take God at His word. With our heart (whole believing) we believe that Jesus is God's Son who died for our sin
on the cross and arose from the grave to live in us as Savior and Lord.

To believe in Jesus will result in confessing that faith with one's mouth.

- Do you acknowledge that you are a sinner?
- Do you believe, by faith, that Jesus, God's Son, died for your sin on the cross and rose again that you might have eternal life?
- Will you now confess Him as your Savior and Lord?

Romans 10:13: "for whoever will call on the name of the Lord will be saved."

This verse says that any person who will call upon the name of Jesus, the Lord, shall be saved.

To call means simply to ask in prayer. **The verse does not require one to know more... do better... clean up one's life... or in any way try to add to what Jesus has done for us.**

Will you now call upon Jesus to save you from your sin so that you can know God's love and forgiveness?

You might pray like this:

"Dear God, I confess that I am a sinner, and I am sorry. I need a Savior. I know I cannot save myself. I believe by faith that Jesus, your Son, died on the cross to be my Savior. I believe He arose from the grave to live as my Lord. I turn from my sin. I ask You, Lord Jesus, to forgive my sin and come into my heart. I trust you as my Savior and receive you as my Lord. Thank you, Jesus, for saving me."

When anyone calls on the Lord in this manner, **that one is saved according to God's Word**. If you pray a prayer of repentance and faith, **you are saved**. **You have God's word on it.**

If you have prayed this prayer to receive Christ as your Lord and Savior, you might want to fill in the following. Perhaps you can keep it in the Bible that you will want to have to teach you all the next steps.

Believing by faith that God loves me and sent His Son, Jesus Christ, to die
for my sin and arise from the grave to live in me, I, _______, do this day,
_______, repent of my sin and accept Jesus Christ as my personal Lord
and Savior. According to the promise of God in Romans

*10:13, I have
called upon His name and have His word for the assurance of
my salvation.* (Special thanks to romanroad.org)

STOP

SPOT CHECK!!

Some readers have skimmed past the last few pages, saying, "Oh, I'm a good person. I'm going to Heaven." Or, "I was baptized when I was little. I've gone to church all my life and I have even taught Sunday School. I must be going to Heaven!"

What was that moment when you knew that you weren't always good, kind, pure, and that you couldn't measure up to anyone's conception of the perfect God? That one moment, even if you were young and don't know the calendar date, when you turned to Jesus Christ and said, "I can't do it, but you can. I'm yours. Period!" If you cannot recall a time when decided to rest your eternity on Jesus Christ, you need to do a spot check. **THIS IS NOT SOMETHING THAT YOU WANT TO PUNT DOWN THE ROAD TO A LATER DATE. THIS IS NOT SOMETHING THAT YOU DON'T WANT TO BE SURE OF!!!**

I'm a preacher's kid, but my dad wasn't in the ministry when I followed my little six-year-old best friend down the aisle in Big Springs, TX. I shook that preacher's hand and he asked me if I "wanted to be saved?" Of course I said yes! I was subsequently baptized. I had no concept of what any of that meant. I had just followed my friend! When I was twelve, the Lord began speaking truth into my heart and I knew, just KNEW, beyond doubt, that, if I died at that time, I would spend eternity away from God. When I was fourteen, my young heart and soul became exhausted with resisting the need to confess that I hadn't given my life to Jesus. (Yes, I was born stubborn.) At fourteen, I stunned my preacher daddy and his entire congregation by responding to the song "Just As I Am" and walking forward to pray with my dad to receive the free gift of salvation through Christ.

Even after Christ gave me new life, preacher's kid or not, I had, as we say in Texas, "a long row to hoe." Married at 18, had my beautiful daughter, Amanda, when I was 20, the beginning of a music career at twenty-two, and a long 13 years of a difficult marriage followed by divorce. Single mom, working mother, college and graduate school student, while all of the above, my dance card was full. And believe me, I didn't feel adequate to dance. My life reflected that, because I spent a season of rebellion against the Lord. I was angry, busy, ill and, in the middle of it all, immersed in a custody battle for my precious only child. It was a dark time and place and I moved far from God. I am very grateful that He called me back!

I knew that, if I were to ever marry again (which was not even ON my list of to-dos), that man would have to be a Christian. Not only a Christian, but one willing to serve the Lord and his family. I had already been through a difficult marriage and a long "winter of the heart," as writer Paula D'Arcy calls it. I was still shrugging off the icicles when I met my husband, Steve. And he was that guy. I thought. And HE thought! He had gone to church. He had been baptized when young. He helped build our church in Missouri and taught Sunday School there and in Nashville. He played drums in the praise band and he booked and managed my music ministry. He had behaved "like a Christian" and he knew all the right answers. HE believed that he was a Christian.

Then, in November of 1999, listening to Pastor Tony Evans on the radio while driving back from Paducah, Kentucky to Nashville, Steve realized that he had never really given his life to Christ. He had never accepted that free gift.

I remember when he walked in the door that night. I was sitting up in bed reading when he came in. There was something so dramatically different in his expression that I had to ask, "What's wrong, Baby?" And my husband of 22 years knelt beside our bed and told me, "I have known all about Jesus for my whole life. Tonight, I met the Man." And Steve has never been the same.

When did you meet that Man? The Man, Christ Jesus? The Quakers have long asked a wise question: If you were to die tonight, do you know for sure that you would go to Heaven? Jesus said, "I am the way, the truth and the life. NO ONE comes to the Father but by Me." John 14:6

John, the beloved disciple of Christ, wrote, "These things I have written to you who believe in the name of the Son of God, that you may know that you have eternal life, and that you may *continue to* believe in the name of the Son of God." (I John 5:13)

<u>NOW IS A GOOD TIME TO STOP AND MAKE SURE!!!!</u>

<u>REFLECTION TIME</u>

One simple question, are you sure?

AND THAT'S ONLY THE BEGINNING!

Having accepted God's gift of salvation, we've only just begun! As you move forward with your new life in Christ, know that growing up in Christ is a process. You are a new creature!

"Therefore, if anyone is in Christ, he is a new creation; **old things have passed away;** behold, all things have become new" (2 Corinthians 5:17)

Jesus told the Jewish leader, Nicodemus, that we "must be born again" (spiritually speaking), through believing on the Lord Jesus Christ and resting our lives in Him. (John 3) The New Testament refers to this newness as being a spiritual "baby."

"You need milk, not solid food! Anyone who lives on milk, being still an infant, is not acquainted with the teaching about righteousness. But solid food is for the mature, who **by constant use** have trained themselves to distinguish good from evil." (Hebrews 5:13,14)

The writer of the book of Hebrews reveals that we are expected to "grow up" to be mature in Christ, spending time "training ourselves" to righteousness.

"Therefore let us move beyond the elementary teachings about Christ and be taken forward to maturity, not laying again the foundation of repentance from acts that lead to death, and of faith in God." Hebrews 6:1

So, as great as beginning a new life in Christ is, there is more and it is not always fun but it is always great and we are to pursue "growing up" into that life and **into the purpose for which we are born!!**

Before we go any further on brokenness that you will experience or have experienced, even now, let's examine that.

There are three phases in our lives as believers. A good thing to remember is the saying, **"We have been saved. We are being saved. We will be saved."**

To explain, our process is:

- <u>**Justification**</u>: **"We have been saved** (out of eternal brokenness)."** When you accept the gift of salvation, **<u>you are forever saved</u>**. You will live in eternity with the Lord. You are **"justified."** You can remember this as **JUST** as **IF I'D** never sinned. Christ took on your sin so that God would see, in you, Jesus Christ.

  - ""For our sakes, HE (God) made HIM (Jesus Christ), who knew no sin to be sin so that, in Him (Jesus Christ) we might become the righteousness of God." (2 Corinthians 5:21)

  - In 1 Corinthians 1:8-9, we find that "He who will sustain you to the end, guiltless in the day of our Lord Jesus Christ. [9] God is faithful, by whom you were called into the fellowship of his Son, Jesus Christ our Lord."

HE WILL NOT DROP YOU!
BUT THIS IS JUST THE START!

- <u>**Sanctification**</u>: **"We are being saved** (from being defeated in brokenness)."

My mom had a placard that read, "God loves me just the way I am and He loves me too much to leave me that way." **God is growing you up**. When a baby is born, she cannot feed herself, change herself, or, in anyway, take care of herself. We are like that. When we are "born again" (John 3), we get eternal life, but we're expected to grow up to be more like Christ. To walk, babies must crawl. Then they stand up – and fall down. They take a step – and fall down. And this goes on and on and on.

When you first learned to ride a bike, did you just jump onto the two wheels and ride off with ease? I doubt it. We all fall. We all skin our knees, bloody our noses and generally learn through failing. **Sanctification** involves learning, through life, hardship, failures and triumphs, to lean on the Lord, who is giving us life, and to **BECOME MORE**.

- The dictionary.com definition for sanctification **is "to make holy; set apart as sacred; consecrate. to purify or free from sin: Sanctify your hearts. to impart religious sanction to; render legitimate or binding: to sanctify a vow. to entitle to reverence or respect. to make productive of or conducive to spiritual blessing."**

- That "goody two-shoes" image that just flashed through your mind – that's not it. To be "set aside" for Christ, to be "made holy," is a process of stepping into the fulfillment of a purposeful, meaningful, fulfilling (lots of "fuls") realization of who God intended you to be **EVEN BEFORE YOU WERE BORN!**

- **Glorification: "We shall be saved** (FOREVER from brokenness)."** Your story has a terrific ending!!! You will live with Him in eternity! Our salvation process will be finished and we will be living, working and ruling forever with Jesus Christ.

- As He was preparing His disciples for His crucifixion, Jesus said, "In My Father's house are many dwelling places; if it were not so, I would have told you; for I go to prepare a place for you. **3** "If I go and prepare a place for you, I will come again and receive you to Myself, that where I am, *there* you may be also." (John 14:2)

- Paul talks about the "glory" of being with Him in Romans 8:18, "I consider that our present sufferings are not worth comparing with the glory that will be revealed in us."

- In the end, we finally will be like Jesus. John, the beloved disciple of Jesus, tells us, "Beloved, now we are children of God, and it has not yet been revealed what we shall be, but we know that, when He is revealed, **we shall be like Him, for we shall see Him as He is."** As the fully God-Man Jesus Christ is! Even John could not imagine how huge that would be!

- You just had another image-flash, didn't you? Floating on a cloud with a harp in hand and (be honest) being bored out of your eternal mind! NOPE! We are created in the image of a Creator God! The possibilities of exciting things we will be doing in His presence are mind-boggling and unlimited!! We are called "joint heirs" with Christ Jesus, Ruler of all ages, so there's exciting work ahead!

REFLECTION TIME

- This is a lot to "unpack." Do you know, without a doubt, that you have met Jesus Christ? Not that you know ABOUT Him, but that you have believed and trusted in Him?

- Can you see Him working in you to become more like Him? To "grow up."

- What are you doing to become more like Him – again, to grow up?
    ◦ Am I studying Scripture?

    ◦ Am I gathering regularly with other committed believers to worship God and learn more about Him?

    ◦ Do I have friends/mentors who can walk this "growing up walk with me?"

- How can you know that, as a little children's Sunday School song says, "He's still working on me?" Or do you think, somewhere deep inside, that He has given up on you? Have YOU given up on you? Who can you talk to about this?

BROKEN, BUT READY TO MOVE ON!

You have life. A new life. A purposeful life. You're ready to move on and grow, just like the Lord wants you to. You want to embrace life in Christ! Right?!? Right! But where to start? HOW???

Be of good cheer, God would never have said that you could do this if He hadn't already given you the resources. These include:

- **The witness and presence in our lives of the Holy Spirit** -the third person of the one God, who is Father, Son and Holy Spirit. Jesus, Himself, promised that, upon Christ's return to sit at the right hand of the Father and represent us, His redeemed, the Holy Spirit would come to dwell within our very beings to teach, guide, convict and grow us.

- **The Bible** – God's Written Revelation to man.
  - Read it daily. It is important to know what the story is in its entirety and what God has done, for all creation, for all mankind, and for you.

  - Find a reading plan. You want to read His book, but, if you haven't started and you go

> to the beginning, you may be like a lot of people who get lost in "so and so begat so and so." There are many "Through The Bible In One Year" plans that will help read through it.
>
> ◦ Find a good translation that also includes study notes. I, personally, use the English Standard Version with its study notes. There are several really good versions that include word-for-word, thought for thought, or general message/paraphrase. In the early days of Bible study, I read through the Phillips paraphrase edition, and, while I don't recommend it for scholarly study, it gave me a deep love for God's Word.

- **Prayer** – Prayer is an ongoing conversation with God through Christ Jesus and empowered by the Holy Spirit. A lot of people put off having those conversations with Him after they've had the initial conversation in which they gave Him their life and He gave them NEW life. It can be daunting. What to do you say to a holy, perfect Creator. Do you need the "thee" and "thou" protocol? What if your grammar and sentence structure is lousy? DON'T WORRY. He's your Father – your Dad. Charles Spurgeon has said,

"A mother can translate baby-talk: she comprehends incomprehensible noises. Even so doth our Father in heaven <u>know all about our poor baby talk</u>, for our prayer is not much better."

A good starting point is the Lord's Prayer and it can provide an outline to kick off your prayers. As it appears in Luke 11:2-4:

2 And he (Jesus) said to them, "When you pray, say (pray this way): "Father, hallowed (holy) be your name.

- ◦ Take time to think of how awesome is God, creator of

all that is but the one who loves you so much!
Your kingdom come.

> [3] Give us this day our daily bread,

- This is a time to ask Him to provide for you and yours, physically and spiritually. For now. Today is all you have, so give Him your today. Bring your needs and concerns to Him. You can "cast all your cares on Him because He cares for you." (1 Peter 5:7)

- Thank Him. He's listening.

"Don't be anxious about anything but, in every situation, with prayer and petition, with thanksgiving, present your requests to God, and the peace of God, **which passes all understanding,** will guard your hearts and your minds in Christ Jesus. (Philippians 4:6,7)

[4] and forgive us our sins, (as) we ourselves forgive everyone who is indebted to us (sins against us). And lead us not into temptation."

- Lead us away from those things, thoughts, desires and situations that would take our eyes off of Jesus.

Oswald Chambers has said, "Prayer is the way that the life of God in us is nourished." There are many resources on praying earnestly and in accordance with God's will. Some of these are:

The Hidden Life of Prayer by David MacIntyre

Face to Face: Praying the Scriptures for Spiritual Growth by Ken Boa

Prayer, The Great Adventure by Dr. David Jeremiah

A Praying Life: Connecting with God in a Distracting World by Paul E. Miller

- **Other believers**
  - You will want to meet with other believers regularly. This is as important for other believers as it is for you. In Romans 12:5, we

are called "one body in Christ and, individually, members (of that body) one of another." We are joined together in salvation by Jesus Christ and we are the physical representation of Him in this world. You may have heard the saying, "You may be the only Jesus some people will ever see." This is true. And you will probably be the one person He has enabled to provide help to other people, or even one person, within the body. **Other believers provide a family that you can lean on.** We fellowship, learn, pray and build one another up in faith.

Finding the right church for you is not always easy, but, as our times get more and more trying, it is important. People often say, "I can worship just as well alone." You'll note that God, Jesus, the apostles and all of the Old Testament saints never said that. Because we are "a body," it is impossible to separate your little body part out and worship in fullness and in truth. Remember Caroline? She had some serious difficulties in following the Lord after a while because she fell away from connecting with other believers. We weren't meant to walk alone! Find believers that you trust to hold you up. Be prepared to hold them up! GROW TOGETHER!!

As you've undoubtedly observed, there are many "churches," many denominations, and many types of service, music, worship, etc. As you study God's Word and spend more time with other believers, you will find that there is a church body somewhere wherein you fit. It may meet in a building, a hotel, a home, whatever, and it may have a handful of members or a large congregation. Just be sure everything taught is in line with the Bible.

- **How do I find the right church?** The following

guidelines may help:

o   **Where Does God Want Me to Serve?**

Prayer is an important part of the process of finding a church. As you seek the Lord's direction, he will give you the wisdom to know where he wants you to fellowship. Be sure to make prayer a priority each step along the way.

o   What Do They Believe?

It's important to understand the doctrinal beliefs of the church before joining. Many people become disillusioned after investing a great deal of time in a church. You can avoid this disappointment by looking closely at the church's statement of faith.

Before joining, be sure the church teaches the Bible effectively. If you're not sure, ask to talk with someone about this. Some churches even offer classes or written material to help you understand the church's doctrine.

o   What Type of Services?

Ask yourself, "Would I feel more freedom to worship through a formal outline, or would I be more comfortable in an informal atmosphere?"

o   What Type of Worship?

Worship is the way we express our love and appreciation to God as well as our awe and wonder at his works and ways. Consider what style of worship will allow you to most freely express adoration to God.

Some churches have contemporary worship music, some have traditional. Some sing hymns, others sing choruses. Some have full bands, others have orchestras and choirs. Some sing gospel, rock, hard rock, etc. **Since worship is a key part of our church experience, be sure to give the style of worship serious consideration.**

o   **What Ministries and Programs Does the Church Have?**

You want your church to be a place where you can connect with other believers. Some churches offer a very simple ministry approach and others extend an elaborate system of classes, programs, productions and more. So, for instance, if you're single and want a church with a single's ministry, be sure to check into this before joining. If you have kids, you'll want to explore the children's ministry.

o   **Does the Size of the Church Matter?**

Smaller church fellowships are usually unable to offer a wide variety of ministries and programs, while larger ones can support an array of opportunities. However, a small church can provide a more intimate, close-knit environment that a large church may not be able to cultivate as effectively. Becoming relational in the body of Christ often requires more effort in a large church. These are things to consider when looking at the size of the church.

o   **What to Wear?**

In some churches t-shirts, jeans, and even shorts are appropriate. In others, a suit and tie or dress would be more appropriate. In some churches, anything goes. So, ask yourself, "What is right for me—dressy, casual, or both?"

o   **Visit Church Websites and Call Before Visiting**

Next, take some time to list specific questions you would want to call and ask before visiting the church. If you take a few minutes each week to do this, it will save you time in the long run. For example, if the youth program is important to you, put that on your list and ask specifically for information about it. Some churches will even mail you an Information Packet or Visitor's Packet, so be sure to ask for these when you call.

You can often get a good feel for a church by visiting its website. Most churches will provide information about how the church got started, doctrinal beliefs, a statement of faith, plus information about vision, ministries and outreaches.

o   Make a List.

Before visiting a church, make a checklist of the most important things you hope to see or experience. Then rate the church according to your checklist when you leave. If you're visiting many churches, your notes will help you compare and decide later. As time passes you may have trouble keeping them straight. This will provide you with a record for future reference.

o   Visit Three Times, And then Ask
Yourself These Questions:

Is this church a place where I can connect with God and worship him freely? Will I learn about the Bible here? Are fellowship and community encouraged? Are people's lives being changed? Is there a place for me to serve in the church and opportunities to pray with other believers? Does the church reach out by sending missionaries and through financial giving and local outreach? Is this where God wants me to be? If you can say yes to these questions, then you've found a good church home.

o   Ask other Christians.

If you still don't know where to begin your search for a church, ask people you know—friends, co-workers, or people you admire, where they go to church.

(Drawn from Fairchild, Mary. "How to Find a Church."
Learn Religions, Apr. 29, 2019, learnreligions.com/
how-to-find-a-church-700487.)

   ◦ Once you find a church, you will want to get involved in some ministry. Remember the part where you were created for a purpose? Growing in Christ involves learning and growing in that purpose. And you have at least one or more gifts that are vital to God's work in the church and in the world.

> "⁴ Now there are varieties of gifts, but the same Spirit; ⁵ and there are varieties of service, but the same Lord; ⁶ and there are varieties of activities, but it is the same God who empowers them all in everyone. ⁷To each is given the manifestation of the Spirit for the common good." (1 Corinthians 12:4-7)

REFLECTION TIME

Make a list of the qualifications you would LIKE to see in a church.

What would you like to see in a gathering of believers that you want to be part of?

Do you think any church can fulfill all of your qualifications?

Why?

Why not?

I KNOW HIM BUT I CAN'T MOVE ON!

You may be really far along the paths outlined above, but the battle is still raging. Even those who love the Lord with all their hearts and want to follow Him faithfully at one point or another will find themselves asking, "Why, Lord? Why can't it just stop for a while?" There are some pains that are temporary and some that are permanent. Why do we have pain when we are so loved by The Great Healer?

I've asked this question myself before. I was in the middle of one of those dark moments when I wrote my song, "Faith." The first two lines are:

> It's dark.
> There's a step I've gotta take and I can't see it.
> My heart
> In confusion is 'bout to break and I can't free it."
> ("Faith" by Kathy Biggers)

At the beginning of this book, I wrote about the church shooting at Sutherland Springs, Texas. As I write this, it is the one-year anniversary of that shooting. The pain of loss continues to ripple even today. Two very beloved personal friends lost loved ones in that shooting and are still reeling with the shock as they continue to try to comfort those who have lost parents, sisters, children. Every time that there is an opportunity to serve in our church or community, these beautiful people are at the forefront. But the pain is still present and searing.

Christmas day, two years ago, we had to make the painful decision to have our beautiful palomino quarter horse put to sleep. Age and illness had led to anguish for him and we, his caretakers, had to decide to put a stop to that anguish. We very much love our pets as family, and this was exceedingly difficult.

Last Christmas, one of my dearest friends had to spend her first Christmas in fifty years without her husband, who had gone on to the Lord earlier that year. This is especially difficult because of the surrounding circumstances. For two years preceding his unexpected illness, she had dealt with a rare lung disease and her life had hung in the balance. She lived longer than predicted with that disease and then God stepped in with a lung transplant. On the way back to their small community from the university hospital where her transplant team had cleared her, she and her husband stopped to celebrate that she would live. At that celebratory lunch, her husband choked on an easy to swallow lunch. They quickly discovered that he had advanced esophageal cancer and he passed shortly thereafter. Daily, she communes with God to find His purpose in that day, the reason that she, who was a death's door, should live while her beloved died.

Another friend experienced that Christmas as a single parent, only getting the beloved child for a portion of this child-focused holiday. So much brokenness around the holiday. Many are dealing with chronic illness and pain. Untold numbers are dealing with abuse or neglect. Again, so much brokenness. And you may have found that the most broken place is inside of you.

<u>REFLECTION TIME</u>

- What's holding you back?

- What "broken pieces" are still causing you pain?

- Are there resentments you aren't ready to let go of? (Just list them and look at them for now.)

NOTES

When you drench your bed with weeping; when you mourn, making loud dole;
When you groan instead of sleeping: 'tis the Dark Night of your Soul.
By betrayal, death, or slander. By hypocrisy or pride.
By what means – it doesn't matter. You feel dark on the inside.

Well, the strength just isn't in you. So it must come from outside.
So you humble what remains of your self-confidence and pride
And you cry out with a wailing shriek, and onwards vainly plod.
You have nothing left. The time is to come face to face with God.

Dark Night of the Soul
antipoetsmartier.wordpress.com

THE "DARK NIGHT OF THE SOUL"

Have you been there? Are you there now? Some of the things you might watch for, if you are, include:

- Feeling a deep sense of sadness, perhaps even despair

- Feeling an acute sense of unworthiness.

- A constant feeling of being lost or "condemned" to a life of suffering or emptiness.

- A painful feeling of powerlessness and hopelessness.

- Feeling that your will and self-control is weakened, making it difficult for you to even move.

- Lack of interest and joy in things that you once enjoyed.

This is the essence of brokenness. The world around you is spinning out of control. The world inside you is just as bad.

You may wonder why I place this AFTER discussing the joys of meeting and knowing Christ, meeting and becoming part of a church body.

It's very simple. Remember what Christ said about having trials in this world. You will.

You will have trials, you will feel broken inside,
and YOU WILL HAVE THE SOURCE OF VICTORY
THROUGH IT ALL!!!

REFLECTION TIME

Are you experiencing any of the symptoms of the "dark night of the soul?" If so, list some of them (for your eyes only, for now).

WHAT'S THE WHY?

There are so many things that can bring us to the point where we are in our "Dark Nights of the Soul."

I will never be able to describe the anguish of my family when my brother, Rick, died from apparent suicide. My father, a dedicated pastor/theologian/teacher and follower of Christ, never totally recovered from the physical impact of the news. My mother dealt with her own loss quietly while trying desperately to ease Dad's misery, and my younger brother and I, along with our families, made every attempt to help when we could while coping with our own emotions. When the evidence began to grow that there was no suicide, but a murder, and that our family would never see justice or closure, the distress settled in and became chronic. We were committed followers of Jesus Christ and the worst of the worse had settled in our lives.

We had to personally come to grips with the universal question, "Why do bad things happen to good people?" To ANY people. More importantly, why do horrible things happen to people who are so committed to living lives that glorify the God who created the universe and who redeemed us? And why is it that the more we serve Him, the harder life seems to be?

Theologians and philosophers have explored this question. Books have been written, debates have been televised, graduate school courses are offered, all centered around this question – if God is good, and if God is all-powerful, why does He let bad things happen? Why doesn't He just stop evil?!?

There are reasons. A few of them, in fact. One is this: there are multiple players in life, players seen and unseen, and each has the will to make choices that affect the other players. People hurt people. Spiritual forces – outside of our understanding – hurt people. We hurt ourselves. As a result this broken world, with jagged rocks, splinters, viruses and germs, hurts people. As my three-year-old granddaughter has said, "It's complicated." Let's break this down.

YOU HAVE AN ENEMY!!!

In His Word, the Bible, God has revealed the earthly story and plan for man and this creation that we see, from beginning to end. Just the earthly part. God had a reason for creating man, for creating YOU, and the path from Genesis to Revelation is a beautiful, logical outline of what our time on earth is about. In addition, the scriptures allow a parting of a curtain to allow us to see the other-dimensional reality that exists in front of us. And one of the things we see is that we have an enemy.

You see, what we can perceive is not all that He created. Scripture tells of the host of beings who observed our creation, who have been given a role in our world, who are eternal and who are also part of our story. One of these, in jealousy and pride, led a revolt that turned a third of these beings against their Creator. In a failed rebellion, these were cast down to earth and continue to rebel and to attempt to foil God's plan for man. Some of them were so successful at spreading depravity and sin among humans and the creation surrounding them that they were bound and "kept in eternal chains under gloomy darkness until the Judgment (Christ's return)." (Jude 1:6) If you would like to understand more of these beings and their role, I recommend beginning with Michael Heiser's book, <u>The Unseen Realm: Recovering the Supernatural Worldview of the Bible.</u>

The warfare tools of the enemy are numerous: deception, lies, sometimes even told by those we trust, betrayals, temptations, depression, anxiety … the list goes on. In telling us about this enemy of man, the Bible says that "we do not wrestle against flesh and blood, but against the rulers, against the authorities, against the cosmic powers over this present darkness, against the spiritual forces of evil in the heavenly places." (Ephesians 6:12) As followers of Christ, we are to "put on the whole armor of God that you may be able to stand against the schemes of the devil." (Ephesians 6:11) 1 Peter 5:8 tells us "be sober-minded; be watchful. Your adversary the devil prowls around like a roaring lion, seeking someone to devour." And the enemy is very deceptive. 2 Corinthians 11:14 tells us that "even Satan disguises himself as an angel of light." The very word, "Satan," means "adversary" or "enemy."

Some of the enemies' tools are so visible that it is frightening! Cable television has made "ghost hunting" a staple since 2004 with "reality" series such as "Ghost Hunters," "Ghost Adventures," and various "Paranormal …" offerings. Though these shows are gimmicky and pseudoscientific, it should alarm any Christian when spirits are invited or commanded to speak. Even more alarming is the habit of "Ghost Adventures" star player, Zak Bagans, and his cohorts to invite the ghosts or demons (they speak of both) to come into them and speak through them. The probability is that these players may, indeed, be opening portals or offering invitations to adversaries that accept the invitation and have no intention of ever leaving. The most recent (2019) advertisements for "Ghost Adventures" even hints at this, superimposing demonic faces over the lead characters' faces and flashing back and forth like the old-fashioned holograph baseball cards. It would be foolish to believe that one plays in the territory of fallen spirits and comes out unharmed.

When I was a teen, my parents thought nothing of giving me a Ouija board for Christmas. After all, it was marketed by Parker Brothers, the game company that gave us Monopoly, Risk, Clue and Trivial Pursuit along with almost 1,800 other games. It is now marketed by Hasbro, makers of G.I. Joe, Transformers, Nerf, My Little Pony, Twister and other games and toys that children everywhere know and love. These game companies kindly advise that the Ouija is recommended only after the advanced age of eight years.

If you don't know about the Ouija, it is a "spirit board" commonly used to communicate with "the dead" (supposedly) and other spirits. The first known use was in China in the 1100s and these boards became common in the spiritualist movement of the 1800s as a means to communicate with dead loved ones. (Remember, the enemy lies. And puts on faces that are familiar to us.) Christians, Catholics and many occult practitioners advise against using the Ouija since doing so may trigger unnatural phenomena that often cannot be contained. In addition, many users of the board have subsequently shown every evidence of being "demonized," either plagued or possessed by outside spirits. Like the invitations of the paranormal TV series players, it is believed to open a portal to another dimension and there is a great deal of evidence that the spiritual enemy of Christ uses it as such. God warns against even playing around with such, as in Deuteronomy 18:10-13:

"There shall not be found among you anyone who burns his son or his daughter as an offering, anyone who practices divination or tells fortunes or interprets omens, or a sorcerer or a charmer or a medium or a necromancer or one who inquires of the dead, for whoever does these things is an abomination to the Lord. And because of these abominations the Lord your God is driving them out before you. You shall be blameless before the Lord your God." (Deuteronomy 18:10)

As I stated, my board was given to me as a game, because that was how it was marketed. The first time that I used it with a friend, the board "took over" and began to spell out the name and life of the "spirit" who was speaking through it, culminating with a promise to appear that evening to us if we would stay together long enough. I hadn't been a Christian for very long and I was not a very mature Christian, but everything in me was repelled by what was happening before our eyes. Needless to say, we did NOT spend that night together at either of our homes and both of us spent a great deal of time praying. We had no training in how to pray for those situations, but we knew that the Lord was going to need to have control over all of it. A few years later, I was stunned to see a woman a few years older than I sitting on the set of a daytime talk show claiming to be the "reincarnated" person whose name and exact details, including location and manner of death exactly matched the "spirit" speaking to us. I'll leave it to the reader to consider how a woman older than I could be the reincarnation of a person who ALSO happened to be a disembodied/dead spirit speaking to the teenaged me. How could both be true? (Hint: they can't.)

The attacks and approaches of the enemy of all that is true and holy are not always as visible or spectacular as some that I have experienced. In fact, they rarely are. These are not natural phenomena. Unfortunately, we see more and more "unnatural" things because we are a generation that values experience over truth. I believe that one of the most powerful phrases that Satan's team has ever coined is, "Your truth is not my truth. That doesn't mean it isn't truth." Not only does that statement defy logic, since truth is truth and not subject to change, but it is a clever diversion from the Truth that spans all generations, all dimensions, all creatures and all time – Jesus Christ, who said, "I am the Way, THE TRUTH, and the Life and NO MAN comes to the Father but BY ME." (John 14:6).

In devotional groups and prayer teams, I have seen beloved friends drawn into a desire for experience over truth, for feeling over growth, for emotion over reality. I have seen "revival" movements spawned out of a need for some emotional endorphin release that looks like psychopathy at best and demonic influence at worst and I have watched families that I deeply treasured fall apart over time because they sought an **experience** over growing in the grace and knowledge of the Lord, in spite of every scriptural warning that God has given us. So the enemy can break God's children even as they think they are chasing Him.

Don't find this alarming. Yes, you have an enemy. **NO, THAT ENEMY DOES NOT HAVE THE POWER TO CONQUER YOU!** No matter who or what this enemy sends against you, you belong to Jesus, who holds ALL THINGS TOGETHER BY HIS WORD, THE WORD OF HIS POWER. (Hebrews 1:3) Jesus has said to his followers, "I have said these things to you that in me you may have peace. In the world *you will have tribulation* (serious troubles). But take heart; **I HAVE OVERCOME THE WORLD."**

<u>REFLECTION TIME</u>

Be assured that the enemy of your soul does not want you to be put back together and to become part of God's Golden Journey for you.

- Looking back, have you participated in any of the occult matters listed in this chapter?

- Have you recognized that these can interfere with your purpose-filled life?

- Have you repented?

- Are there areas where you feel the enemy's influence but where you haven't invited it and don't want it?

Check the resources listed in the back of this book, in particular, <u>The Invisible War</u>, Randall, 2013.

YOU HAVE A VICTORY!

You have an enemy, but you have a Savior who has already defeated that enemy. But understand, that does not mean that you have no role in the battle. Suit up and prepare to take action!

As noted above, we are told that we are to be sober-minded and watchful. We are also told to be engaged in the battle! Ephesians 6:10-18 gives the Christ-follower the "battle plan."

Finally, **be strong in the Lord and in the strength of his might. Put on the whole armor of God, that present darkness**, against the spiritual forces of evil in the heavenly places.

Therefore take up the whole armor of God, that you may be able to withstand in the evil day, **and having done all, to stand firm**. Stand therefore, **having fastened on the belt of truth, and having put on the breastplate of righteousness, and, as shoes for your feet, having put on the readiness given by the gospel of peace. In all circumstances take up the shield of faith, with which you can extinguish all the flaming darts of the evil one; and take the helmet of salvation, and the sword of the Spirit, which is the word of God, praying at all times in the Spirit, with all prayer and supplication**. To that end, keep alert with all perseverance, making supplication for all the saints. (Ephesians 6:10-17)

As you can tell, a Christian has no need to lie down and play dead when things go badly. Things WILL go badly sometimes. As people often shrug and say, "That's life." But, remember, Christ told us not to be afraid because He has OVERCOME! Therefore, we are to be Overcomers with and because of Him. We are to keep moving forward. Note that there is no armor for the back. We're supposed to face our life issues and overcome.

Got.questions.org has an excellent description of how we are to overcome and we will look at that description after we examine more reasons we suffer brokenness while living in this world.

YOU ARE TO OVERCOME

I have been privileged to work with women who had suffered abuse, violence, rape, incest, drug and alcohol addiction and more. As they shared their stories and their walk to recovery, day by day, I was amazed at how much horror people can go through and how completely Jesus can reach into their lives and begin healing them. **Day by day**. A walk from wreckage to joy. **Day by day.**

I have watched as friends emerged from the saddest of places to stand tall and victorious and to use what they have learned in their dark places to help others. The people I value most, the people who seem most alive, are people who have literally faced the demons of hell, leaned on the Spirit of the Living God, and emerged as MORE. More alive! More mature! Sweeter. I've learned from these people. I LOVE these people!

These people are <u>OVERCOMERS!!!</u>

The Bible has a lot to say about being an overcomer. The term *overcomer* is especially prominent in the book of Revelation, where Jesus encourages His people to remain steadfast through trials (Revelation 2:26; 3:21; 21:7). First John 5:4–5 says, "<u>For whatever is born of God overcomes the world</u>; and this is the victory that has overcome the world—our faith. Who is the one who overcomes the world, but he who believes that Jesus is the Son of God?"

Overcomers are followers of Christ who successfully resist the power and temptation of the world's system. An overcomer is not sinless, but holds fast to faith in Christ until the end. <u>He does not turn away when times get difficult</u> ... Overcoming requires complete dependence upon God for direction, purpose, fulfillment, and strength to follow His plan for our lives (Proverbs 3:5–6; 2 Corinthians 12:9).

The Greek word most often translated "overcomer" stems from the word *nike* which, according to *Strong's Concordance*, means "to carry off the victory. The verb implies a battle." The Bible teaches Christians to recognize that the world is a battleground, not a playground. God does not leave us defenseless. Ephesians 6:11–17 describes the armor of the Lord available to all believers. Scattered throughout this narrative is the admonition to "stand firm." <u>Sometimes all it takes to overcome temptation is to stand firm and refuse be dragged into it</u>. James 4:7 says, "<u>Resist the devil and he will flee from you.</u>" An overcomer is one who resists sin no matter what lures Satan uses.

The apostle Paul wrote eloquently of overcoming in Romans 8:35–39. He summarizes the power believers have through the Holy Spirit to overcome any attacks of the enemy. Verse 37 says, "<u>In all these things we are more than conquerors through him who loved us.</u>"

Overcoming is often equated with enduring. Jesus encouraged those who followed Him to "endure to the end" (Matthew 24:13). A true disciple of Christ is one who endures through trials by the power of the Holy Spirit. An overcomer clings to Christ, no matter how high the cost of discipleship. Hebrews 3:14 says, "We have come to share in Christ, if indeed we hold our original conviction firmly to the very end."

In the book of Revelation, Jesus promised great reward to those who overcome. Overcomers are promised that they will eat from the Tree of Life (2:7), be unharmed by the second death (2:11), eat from hidden manna and be given a new name (2:17), have authority over the nations (2:26), be clothed in white garments (3:5), be made a permanent pillar in the house of God (3:12), and sit with Jesus on His throne (3:21). Jesus warned that holding fast to Him would not be easy, but it would be well worth it. In Mark 13:13 He says, "You will be hated by all for my name's sake. But the one who endures to the end will be saved" (ESV). **We have the guarantee of Jesus that, if we are His, we will be able to endure to the end and His rewards will make it all worthwhile.** (Used by permission. https://www.gotquestions.org/Bible-overcomer.html)

So this is one of the reasons that this enemy still gets to hang around for awhile longer: that we might become Overcomers with Christ. That we might be more like Him! **THAT'S A VIC-TORY!!!!**

BUT WAIT! WE HAVE ANOTHER ENEMY???

You do have another enemy. As Pogo said:

I cannot recount how many times I have heard someone moan, "Why do these things happen to me? WHY ME?" Sometimes that is a hard question to answer. Sometimes the answer is so obvious that it's ridiculous. BECAUSE WHEN WE DO THE WRONG STUFF, WE GET THE WRONG RESULTS. WHEN WE DO THE WRONG STUFF OVER AND OVER AGAIN, WE GET THE WRONG RESULTS OVER AND OVER AGAIN!!!!!

I have sometimes put my trust in the wrong friends. Because of my own youth and spiritual immaturity, I have had wrong reasons for choosing a mate. Pride and its opposite/twin, insecurity, have led me to make some horrible choices in companions, actions and thoughts. In those thoughts, I dishonored God, my Father. Sometimes we follow the wrong leaders.

SOMETIMES WE JUST MAKE BAD CHOICES!!

How often do we hear, "Actions have consequences?" Our choices have consequences and, sometimes, consequences are painful. They may lead into abuse, both received and delivered. They may lead into physical pain and disability. They may (and probably will) leave us feeling distant from or abandoned by God! He never leaves us or stops loving us, but, sometimes, it just feels as if He has.

As we grow more and more into what Jesus wants us to be (which is like Him), we grow more irritated with our own problem behavior. I look back at so many of the things that I've done and want to weep. There are so many ways that I have dishonored the Lord, my God. So many consequences stemming from selfishness and my own sin. Thank God He doesn't leave me wallowing in that!

Even the Apostle Paul said,

"[15] For I do not understand my own actions. For I do not do what I want, but I do the very thing I hate. [16] Now if I do what I do not want, I agree with the law, that it is good. [17] So now it is no longer I who do it, but sin that dwells within me. [18] For I know that nothing good dwells in me, that is, in my flesh. For I have the desire to do what is right, but not the ability to carry it out. [19] For I do not do the good I want, but the evil I do not want is what I keep on doing." (Romans 7:15-19)

Being born again, a Christian, forever belonging to and living with God, does NOT mean you won't sin anymore. **It means that you become aware of sinning.** And the more you understand about how He wants you to live, the more you understand when you blow it. And you want NOT TO BLOW IT! BECAUSE BLOWING IT HAS CONSEQUENCES! We hurt other people! We hurt ourselves. We sit in self-pity and become useless to the Kingdom of God.

AND SOMETIMES WE JUST MAKE NOT-SO-
BAD BUT WRONG CHOICES!!

I have mentioned how my husband, Steve, came to Christ after we were married. He met Christ Jesus in 1999. He got really, really busy for the Lord. As time went on, he became involved in the "Building and Grounds" committee, spending countless hours on church projects, travelling great distances to acquire needed materials, ultimately neglecting home needs between the demands of professional and church work.

In 2013, that came to an abrupt halt. Steve was in the middle of a very hectic photography season in his national photography business and he had multiple projects going on at church, as well as a burgeoning local awning business.

He left Nashville on Wednesday morning to drive to a town just south of St. Louis, Missouri to pick up supplies for one of those church projects. Behind his pickup truck, he pulled a long trailer. Late that afternoon, I got a call from his phone.

"Hey, darlin'!" I answered.

On the other end, a short hesitation and then, "Mrs. Biggers?"

My heart stopped as I heard the rest. Emergency crews were on the scene and using the "Jaws of Life' to cut my husband from the cab of his truck. They were going to transport him to Cape Girardeau, Missouri. After he arrived, details began to be fleshed out. He had been involved in an accident wherein his truck was clipped and he had flipped over three times at 75 miles per hour with his trailer being flung hundreds of feet from his truck. The only thing that kept him from being in the middle of oncoming traffic was one tire caught on one steel pole holding up the retaining wire.

As I rushed toward Cape Girardeau, I got a call that they were going to life-flight him to Barnes Jewish Medical Center in St. Louis. I immediately headed in that direction and, as I travelled, I was told that tornadoes were ahead of me and, in Missouri, had grounded the Life Flight. They were going to transport him by ambulance.

The next few days at Barnes Jewish were grounded in prayer and uncertainty. His back was broken in two places, with the uppermost fracture appearing to be sheared straight through. He had other minor fractures and his left hand was badly injured. Surgery and partial or total paralysis loomed.

Prayer warriors all over the world began to pray for my husband! Praise God, further MRIs indicated that a long period in a hardshell body and neck brace might suffice rather than surgery and the "sheared" vertebrae was not broken through. The potential for paralysis was still there and complete regimen and physical therapy adherence would be required.

After a few nights of lying immobile in a hospital bed, while I was getting one of my few short sleeps, Steve began to weep and have what he describes as his "pity party."

"Why? Why, God? Why me? Why now?"

Steve will tell you that he has rarely actually had a moment when he HEARD God. As in God's voice. But at this time, the Lord spoke to Him.

"Steve, be still. Be still and know that I am God."

Steve stilled. A short while later, he heard, very clearly, "You have been running FOR Me for a long time now. But you haven't bothered to WALK with Me."

That moment became the second life changer for Steve.

Not walking with Jesus is a crippling sin. Not learning more about Jesus is a growth-stunting sin. Not praying, spending time loving and knowing Jesus is a life-denying sin. Not serving is a life-halting sin.

See, there are many things we can DO that are visibly against God. But once we are in His body of believers, we are to be in His Presence and His service, and we are to be serving one another. Not doing so is staying as a baby. Refusing to grow up in Christ is just wrong!

OKAY, SO WHAT DO WE DO?

We confess our sin to the Lord. We ask for forgiveness and He promises forgiveness. Our sins won't lead to losing our salvation. That bears repeating: NONE OF OUR SINS LEAD TO LOSING OUR SALVATION!

"Therefore if any man is in Christ, he is a new creature; the old things are passed away; behold, new things have come." (2 Corinthians 5:17).

We aren't refurbished or remodeled versions of our own selves. WE ARE NEW CREATURES. The OLD creature is gone, and even if you begin to act in old ways, you can't become that creature again. Which makes our return to old behaviors, behaviors that don't look like Christ, more painful to us and to Him.

So, you gossip. It gets back to the subject of your gossip, blows up in your face and you lose people's respect. You ask forgiveness and you receive it. But the consequence is that you've lost people's respect. You think or say bad things about someone and, spiritually, you and/or someone is hurt. You indulge in road rage and someone gets hurt. Or just gets angrier and angrier, so blood pressure spikes. You smoke; you get lung cancer and wonder why, oh, why? You ask forgiveness. But you smoked and a predictable consequence is likely cancer. You don't take care of the body God gave you and you get sick.

The possibilities are numerous. Christians can still fall far and hard. They can neglect or mistreat their children and their children will be taken from them or grow to hate them. They can neglect their relationships and end up with none. They can cheat on their spouses, either physically or mentally and emotionally, with another person or with the images on books, movies, magazines or the internet. The consequences are mental anguish, loss of the trust of the spouse, broken marriages and heartbreak. We can simply allow distance and apathy to stunt our spiritual lives!

There are so many ways we self-destruct! Still, God forgives the earnest repentance of a person. But, since He is in the business of "growing us up" to fellowship with Him and be like Him, He does not take away the consequences.

So who is the enemy here? Do we say, with the late comedian, Flip Wilson, "The devil made me do it?"

Nope. Nope. Nope. The Apostle Paul could be paraphrased as saying, "I have met the enemy and he is me."

Feeling hopeless yet? Paul could have felt hopeless. As he said,

"Wretched man that I am! Who will deliver me from this body of death?" But he answered his own question, Thanks be to God through Jesus Christ our Lord!" (Romans 7: 24 and 25)

Go back and read about overcoming. Even when we are our own worst enemy, Jesus Christ, our Lord, makes our failing known to us so that we can bring the failing to Him, ask forgiveness, GROW UP and OVERCOME!!! God isn't growing sissies. He is growing co-rulers!

AND THAT'S ANOTHER VICTORY!!!

<u>REFLECTION TIME</u>

- Where am I my worst enemy?
- Where have I made choices that have me stuck where I am now?
- Am I ready to move on? If so, can I accept that my past has brought me to where I am today but God wants me to move to where I am supposed to be?
- What's my next move?

Remember Paul's encouragement: "This one thing I do. Forgetting what lies behind, reaching out to what lies ahead, I press on to The Goal ... to WIN THE PRIZE OF GOD'S HIGH CALLING IN CHRIST JESUS!" (Philippians 3:13)

BUT WHY ME?

So why would these things happen to you? You have given your life to Jesus. Wouldn't things be easy now? Little kids in Sunday School have been singing, "Now I am happy all the time" for decades. Shouldn't I be happy all the time? Ummm, not likely (and we shouldn't teach our kids songs that set up unrealistic expectations.)

- In all cases, the suffering (even suffering unto death) is *temporary*, and it fades into nothing when compared to the promised kingdom (2 Cor 4:17, Phil 3:8).

- In all cases, the temporary suffering of the righteous can *honor God* (Matt 5:11-12).

WHY ME?

- In a word – GRACE!

- God has planned, from the beginning of time, to demonstrate His Grace in your life!! John Piper has stated that "The goal of the entire history of redemption is to bring about the praise of the glory of the grace of God." (https://www.desiringgod.org/messages/the-suffering-of-christ-and-the-sovereignty-of-god).

- "[God] saved us and called us to a holy calling, not because of our works but because of his own purpose and grace, which he gave us [that is, he gave us this grace] in Christ Jesus before the ages began." (2 Timothy 1:9)

- ◦ "Molding you and shaping you to be what He needs you to be to further His Kingdom and draw people to Him."

- ◦ As you stand firm in His truth in the middle of the worst, you may lose some things but you gain so much.

For each of us, it is:

- To help you fully appreciate what Christ went through for you.

- In your relationships with one another, to have the same mindset as Christ Jesus:

- ◦ Who put aside EVERYTHING for you.

- ◦ [6] Who, being in very nature God, did not consider equality with God something to be used to his own advantage; [7] rather, he made himself nothing by taking the very nature of a servant, being made in human likeness. [8] And being found in appearance as a man, he humbled himself by becoming obedient to death—even death on a cross!

- ◦ Who endured IMMENSE SUFFERING for you.

- To "grow you up." become more like Jesus as we move through life. Trials and growth lead us to:

"Put off your old self, which belongs to your former manner of life and is corrupt through deceitful desires, and to be renewed in the spirit of your minds, and to put on the new self, created after the likeness of God in true righteousness and holiness." (Ephesians 4:22-24)

- To help someone who is walking where you've walked, hurting where you've hurt, crying where you've cried, bleeding where you've bled. To be the physical hands and voice through which the Lord can reach and love others.

HERE IS THE CRUX OF IT ALL, THE IMPORTANT THING: CHRIST IS WORKING THROUGH EVERYTHING WE ARE, EVERY BROKENNESS AND ACTIONS OVER WHICH WE HAVE HAD NO CONTROL, TO BRING US INTO ETERNAL RELATIONSHIP, FELLOWSHIP AND PARTNERSHIP WITH HIM. FOREVER AND EVER!

"The saying is trustworthy, for: If we have died with him, we will also live with him; if we endure, we will also reign with him."

2 Timothy 2:11–13

<u>REFLECTION TIME</u>

- Are you willing to examine the broken places you've avoided seeing?

- What scriptures from this chapter will you use to see Christ's work in your life?

- As you look at and pray about where you feel or have felt broken, what has God done in the middle of it all? At the end of it all? What do you think He might do?

DON'T DO THIS ONE THING!!

DON'T GO IT ALONE!

I admit it. When I'm falling apart, I feel totally alone. Mentally, I know that the Father has never left me or forsaken me. He has said so:

"Be strong and courageous, do not be afraid or tremble at them, for the LORD your God is the one who goes with you. He will not fail you or forsake you." (Deuteronomy 31:6)

But, honestly, knowing in my head is not the same as knowing in my heart. When I am in pain, my heart sometimes feels totally isolated from the world. Hopeless. Lonely. Redeemed but drifting. Surrounded by family and loved ones. And alone.

I've spoken with many who have just gone through or are in the midst of some of the darkest "nights of the soul."

And being vulnerable, being transparent IS SCARY!!!! We don't want to bother anyone and we don't want to be more vulnerable than we already are. If you're like me, you have felt small, stupid, and hopeless for being in that situation that has you defeated. How can anyone understand? Why should they? And why should they care? Someone will. Speak to pastors of the churches that interest you or where you have landed. There is someone who will care and who is looking for someone to care for them.

True, you may not actually have connections and wouldn't know where to start. I would suggest someone working in the church office. They are almost always extremely caring and helpful.

Most people would start with the pastor and, in small churches, that might be the right path. In larger churches, that might be more difficult. On Sundays, pastors work. As a preacher's kid, trust me. Pastors WORK! And it is difficult to get their time because up to HUNDREDS of people want their time. For them, as well as for us, time is a finite commodity and pastors have to work in their church families AND their own families (which, by the way, should come first). I have, both in ministries and in churches where I was a member, found some pastors who seemed "too busy" and could be seen as "blowing off" the hurting, which can be painful if you are hurting and need someone. If you find that to be true and you get a truly cavalier response, you need to find a different family. But you do NOT need to give up. God has someone to come alongside you. Someone to whom you can make a difference.

 "God sets the solitary in families; He brings out those who are bound into prosperity; but the rebellious dwell in a dry land. Psalm 68:6

Bear one another's burdens, and so fulfill the law of Christ.
     - Galatians 6:2

We who are strong have an obligation to bear with the failings of the weak, and not to please ourselves.
     - Romans 15:1

Let each of you look not only to his own interests, but also to the interests of others.

- Philippians 2:4

A friend loves at all times, and a brother is born for adversity.
- Proverbs 17:17

Do not neglect to do good and to share what you have, for such sacrifices are pleasing to God. Hebrews 13:16

"Therefore encourage one another and build up one another, just as you also are doing" (1 Thessalonians 5:11).

"God has so composed the body, giving more abundant honor to that member which lacked, so that there may be no division in the body, but that the members may have the same care for one another. And if one member suffers, all the members suffer with it" (1 Corinthians 12:24-26).

Don't go it alone. God has a plan for you. A wonderful plan! And it includes other people. You need them! They need you!!

For God to bring you through this "kintsugi," this Golden Journey, you have to take the first step. Then you must keep walking!

Your brokenness can be something beautiful! Step into it. Step into Jesus.

I don't know you, but I can honestly tell you I love you. Jesus loves you. Someone else will, too. You can leave me a message at biggersministries.com. Be blessed!

<u>REFLECTION TIME</u>

This page is for one thing only – your "people" list.

- Who do you know that you can trust and who will walk with you?

- If that list is empty or too short, who would you LIKE to trust and walk with?

- What one person can you ask to be your partner in this walk toward the beauty that God is making from your brokenness?

- ASK

I pray that God will richly bless your life as you move closer and closer into His embrace.

One of my favorite mental images is this: when asked how much Jesus loved me, he said, "This much!" and he stretched out his arms and died.

Grace and Peace be with you.

Kathy Biggers

RESOURCES

Suicide Prevention Hotline   Call 988

To contact us:
https://biggersministries.com

General

Brown, Tammy. *Healed and Set Free.* 2003, Calvary Chapel of Idaho Falls.

Coad, Norman. *The Divided Soul: A Biblical, Theological & Psychological Approach to Therapy and Healing of Dissociative Identity Disorder*
CoadWordBooks.com.

Frangipane, Francis. *The Three Battlegrounds Revised.* 2006, Arrow Publications.

Randall, Rob. *Lies That Kill: The Supernatural Battle for Truth.* 2013, 21st Century Press.

Randall, Rob. *The Invisible War: Living In Victory Over the Enemy.* 2013, 21st Century Press.

Roberts, Diane. *Betrayal and Beyond: Fashioning a Courageous Heart.* 2019, Pure Desires Ministries International.

MacIntyre, David. *The Hidden Life Of Prayer._*1993, Bethany House Publishers.

Boa, Ken. *Face to Face: Praying the Scriptures for Spiritual*

Growth. 1997, Zondervan.

Jeremiah, David. *Prayer, the Great Adventure.* 2004, Multnomah.

Miller, Paul E; Powlison, David. *A Praying Life: Connecting with God in a Distracting World, 2nd Edition.* 2017, NavPress.

https://www.celebraterecovery.com/
https://www.overcomersoutreach.org/
https://www.harvestusa.org/
https://tlgn.org/ (The LifeGivers Network)
https://www.christian-works.org/
https://www.hopefortheheart.org/
https://christiananswers.net/
https://proverbs31.org/
https://thegritandgraceproject.org/

Grief
https://www.hopeforthebrokenhearted.com/
https://www.christian-works.org/grief/griefworks/
https://www.christian-works.org/

When hurt by sexual addiction/addicts
https://2.bebroken.com/
https://www.celebraterecovery.com/
https://www.overcomersoutreach.org/

Self-injury/cutting/eating disorders
https://christiananswers.net/q-eden/cutting.html
https://freedomfromed.com/christian-recovery/
https://christiananswers.net/q-eden/
eatingdisorders.html
https://christiananswers.net/q-eden/cutting.html
http://www.psyke.org/
http://www.self-injury.org/

https://www.eatingsdisorders.com/christian-based-eating-disorder-treatment/

Divorce
https://www.divorcecare.org/

Abortion
http://hopeafterabortion.com/
http://www.saveone.org/

Human trafficking
World Relief Fort Worth
We are Cherished - Reaching Out to Women in the Sex Industry
Mosaic Family Services
Refugee Services of Texas - Fort Worth Office
Texas Youth and Runaway Hotline
Texas Association Against Sexual Assault
US Immigration and Customs
Letot Center Safe House for Exploited Women
Human Trafficking Search
International Rescue Committee - Dallas
TraffickStop
The Freedom Commons
Treasured Vessels Foundation